The Bentley Story

The Bentley Story

Reg Abbiss

The
History
Press

Published in the United Kingdom in 2014 by
The History Press
The Mill · Brimscombe Port · Stroud · Gloucestershire · GL5 2QG

British Library Cataloguing in Publication Data
A catalogue record for this book is available from the British
Library.

Hardback ISBN 978-0-7509-5462-4

Typesetting and origination by The History Press
Printed in India

Cover illustrations. Front: 1929 Speed Six, originally a Park Ward
saloon, now carrying a Vanden Plas roadster body; *back*: the
classic modern Bentley grille fitted to a 2002 Azure drophead
coupé.

CONTENTS

ACKNOWLEDGEMENTS

To the many world-class engineers and craftsmen and women of Bentley Motors and Rolls-Royce Motor Cars, who built the finest motor cars in the world.

Photographs and illustrations courtesy of:

Bentley Motors
Rolls-Royce Motor Cars
W.O. Bentley Memorial Foundation
Alan Bodfish
Larry S. Glenn
Bonhams: Simon Clay, Pawel Litwinski and Rupert Banner
Frank Allocca
Sabu Advani
Graham Hull
Christopher Abbiss
Marian Savage

Bentley – a name revered by driving enthusiasts for almost a century – occupies an exalted place in the automotive firmament. But the journey has not been without scary events when financial troubles threatened survival.

In 1931, 12-year-old Bentley Motors, having carved a glorious racing reputation with a record string of victories at Le Mans and Brooklands, went under in the Depression and was bought by Rolls-Royce, which itself succumbed in 1971. The dominant aerospace side of the company collapsed through cost overruns on an advanced technology engine for the Lockheed Tri-Star jetliner, and was bailed out by the British Government. The car division was spun off as an independent company.

After this narrow escape, the Rolls-Royce and Bentley car makers flourished for twenty years, until high production costs and a devastating recession demanded huge changes or oblivion. Bentley, with new, exciting performance cars, kept the firm afloat, paying Rolls-Royce back for its rescue half a century earlier. But it was evident that a boutique company

▼ Aggressive vintage Bentley – 1925 Continental Supersports.

painstakingly making handcrafted cars could not survive without partnering with a larger group. There was a bruising takeover battle in 1998 between the German powerhouses, Volkswagen and BMW, and Rolls-Royce and Bentley separated.

With deep-pocketed parents, they thrive today, still dedicated to the commitment to excellence laid down by their founders, the gifted engineers Walter Bentley and Henry Royce.

Walter Owen Bentley was born in 1888 into a financially comfortable family in London's St John's Wood; this was very different to the circumstances of Frederick Henry Royce, who had to work from the age of 10 to help his widowed mother make ends meet.

Both started out as apprentices, dreaming of great things like engineering the best cars in the world. And they did. After years of endeavour and success, their companies came together to create a legendary automotive dynasty that endured for almost three-quarters of a century.

Royce made refined, quiet, reliable motor cars with names like Ghost and Phantom that were hailed as the best in the world. Bentley built powerful, hefty touring cars that could double as racing machines and burn up any road in Europe. They were piloted by aggressive drivers who blasted to victory on European motor-racing circuits.

These were the Bentley Boys, hard-driving young men who enjoyed London society high life and hustled their growling cars to Le Mans or Brooklands to joust with other adventurous drivers at insane speeds on sharp corners and steep banking.

Open cars had none of the safety equipment mandated today – leather helmets were the norm. Safety was not an issue, nor money. Excitement and

◄ At home on the race track as well as a country road; a 1929 supercharged 4½-litre Bentley.

◄ Return to Le Mans. Two modern-day Bentley racers, averaging 133mph, came first and second in the 2003 Le Mans race, seventy-three years after the last Bentley win in 1930. Number 7, the winner, 'on the esses'.

► The revered Bentley Continental name was applied to a spectacular coach-built convertible, for drivers who desired craftsmanship and luxurious interior but opted for a profile lower than exemplified by the Rolls-Royce Corniche.

the prestige of driving for Bentley were the rewards.

With names like Woolf, Tim, Clive and Sammy, the Bentley Boys won the most demanding contest in the world – the Le Mans 24 Hours endurance race – five times in six years. And they made Brooklands their own, where Bentley won its first race in 1921 and many other record-setting events afterward. Bentleys dominated international motor racing for years and became the world's most admired and feared sporting cars.

But even the best party can lose steam, and after being acquired by Rolls-Royce, Bentley Motors' unique identity was clouded by being mostly Rolls-Royce clones. Until the R-Type Continental appeared in the early 1950s, enthusiasts had to make do with a Royce fitted with a Bentley radiator and Flying B insignia.

In the 1980s, half a century after the takeover, Rolls-Royce had an epiphany. They speculated that a serious Bentley revival could attract young buyers who sought a sporty luxury car and top-notch engineering without the establishment image of a Rolls-Royce. Bentley regained its high performance 'driver's car' identity with powerful turbocharged engines and firm suspensions. Talk about prescience or divine guidance! A range of exciting, sporting motor cars with distinctive Bentley grilles, cockpit-like interiors, handcrafted veneers and Connolly leather triggered a Bentley renaissance.

The surge developed as Rolls-Royce Motor Cars was running into financial problems and the cavalry charge of Bentley super cars saved the company from going under. Soon they were outselling Rolls-Royce by several to one. Bentley was back, and today they arguably produce the finest range of stylish, technically advanced, sporting luxury cars.

The Bentley Story may sound like something from a boy's adventure paper, but it happens to be true: an exhilarating story of which Britons can be proud. I hope you enjoy it.

Reg Abbiss
Autumn 2014

◀ Bentley performance road car: 1930 Corsica Speed Six.

So, what's special about a Bentley apart from costing a lot of money? For a start, the drivers are different – if you ignore the affluence that they and Rolls-Royce owners generally have in common. Most are motoring enthusiasts, eager to drive a sporty performance car and are usually perhaps more adventurous than Rolls-Royce owners in lifestyle and tastes, in wine and women. This does not characterise them all, of course, but, historically and emotionally, most Bentley owners probably wouldn't argue with that.

The man to whom they tip their hats is Walter Owen Bentley, a quiet, unassuming man who built powerful racers masquerading as robust road cars that could outrun just about anything on the road. He created a motoring image so strong that it survived near-death experiences to rise, phoenix-like, and retake its special place while embracing a new generation.

He shared many talents with Henry Royce, another motoring pioneer: both

➤ Walter Owen Bentley, whose engineering achievements earned him a special place in aviation, automotive and racing history.

➤➤ Still a beauty: 1927 3-litre with an original Vanden Plas tourer body. (W.O. Bentley Memorial Foundation)

1926 Speed Six. Originally a Park Ward saloon, but now a Vanden Plas tourer. (Larry S. Glenn)

were talented designers and mechanical visionaries passionate about engineering excellence. Their companies built the finest cars in the world, despite bumps along the way, forged reputations for honesty and integrity, and maintained a commitment to producing the very best.

An imaginative engineer, Bentley, like Royce, got his early mechanical training as a railway workshop apprentice. Fascinated by locomotives, he left boarding school at age 16 for the Great Northern Railway in the gritty town of Doncaster, Yorkshire. This was markedly different from the comfortable world he knew as a child in a posh part of London. He filed metal rods and worked in the foundry for the first year, then moved to the engine shops, overhauling steam engines. At the age of 21 he was a footplate fireman and a 400-mile Leeds to London round trip had him shovelling up to 7 tons of coal into the firebox. The day started at 5.30 a.m. and usually ran to twelve hours or longer.

He bought a motorcycle and competed in the 1909 Isle of Man Tourist Trophy race, which ended quickly – he crashed on lap one. But he persevered, finishing second in a race at Brooklands and going on to win three gold medals in track and road events. Later Bentley drivers were to dominate Brooklands, writing much of its history and breaking many speed records along the way.

Did you know?

W.O. Bentley's company car, a 1930 8-litre, is still on the road. In 2012 it completed the week-long China Rally of International Classic Cars.

The 1931 4½-litre supercharged Le Mans tourer/racer that was auctioned for £3 million in California in 2013. (Bonhams/Paul Litwinski)

He left the railway to work in a taxi service shop in London, then went into business with his brother in 1912 – the year the *Titanic* sank. They opened a car showroom in Mayfair, and Walter determined that motor sports, using alloy pistons, could build the business. He won hill climbs and races, and this included setting a speed record at Brooklands.

Realising that alloy pistons could increase aero-engine power, he designed an engine for British fighter planes – the Bentley Rotary 1 – which was in production as the First World War began. This was followed with a larger version, the BR2. He was then in his mid-twenties. The £8,000 he was paid for the aero-engine design work helped finance the foray into the car business.

Bentley's engineering passion drove him to design and build fast, reliable sports tourers. In January 1919, he and two engineering colleagues, Frederick Burgess

Did you know?
Aluminium pistons, which operated in cast-iron wet cylinder lines, were precisely matched in pairs and machined to within half of one-one-thousandth of an inch of perfect roundness.

and Harry Varley, started work on the first Bentley car with an easily serviced 3-litre engine. The engine and chassis were ready by October, fronted by a tall, bull-nosed radiator and wire-mesh grille that would become Bentley hallmarks. An *Autocar* magazine road test praised the car as having tractability and great speed usually found on machines built for racing.

A small factory at Cricklewood, North London, became the assembly works; most components were also made there because manufacturers showed little interest in supplying a small company. The first chassis did not reach a customer until 1921.

Like Rolls-Royce, it was many years before Bentley offered customers a complete car. He built the chassis and mechanicals to which some of the finest coachbuilders of the day added their artistry – hence the many attractive individual designs still on the road. All the cars bore the famous Flying B, which still proudly adorns every radiator, and Bentley had such faith in his cars that he gave a five-year warranty.

Walter Bentley used any excuse not to act like a businessman, preferring to work on technical development, testing prototypes and conferring with engineers at Cricklewood. His racing and hands-on engineering experience resulted in cars that

Did you know?

Bentleys are admired for many beautiful body styles. The reason for so many is that until 1946, the engine, chassis and running gear were sent to specialist coachbuilders chosen by an owner, who then designed and crafted the coachwork.

were close to being detuned racers. Nobody quite accepted that it was coincidental that high-performance road cars happened to be able to thrash competitors at Le Mans. Chassis generally believed to be strong enough to carry a London bus were married to muscular engines of tremendous power – up to 8 litres – setting Bentleys apart for speed, stamina and reliability.

> Evolving shapes. Montage by Graham Hull of seventy years of Bentleys, 1929–98.

>> When vintage Bentleys get together. Hunting as a pack on a heritage drive.

'W.O.', as Walter Owen Bentley was known, had a mission statement: 'To build a good car, a fast car, the best in its class.' And he made memorable cars that still turn heads to this day. You may remember the Blower-Bentley (blower having a supercharger fixed to the front) driven by John Steed in the *Avengers* television series. Such classics are pursued by collectors, some perhaps wistfully trying to recapture the urges of their youth, and huge sums are offered when one comes up for sale.

In August 2013, a notable tourer/racer was auctioned in California for £3 million. It was a 1931 4½-litre Blower-Bentley, one of only three built to Le Mans specifications, and capable of 125mph. It was the inspiration of Bentley Boy Tim Birkin and had been owned by Roger Noble's family for more than half a century. After intense bidding, it was bought by a European.

Back in the seventies, when most buyers opted for a Rolls-Royce as a tangible symbol of success, few Bentleys were to be seen at the Crewe factory – where they had been built since 1946. Spotting one, a factory visitor murmured: 'Ah, a Bentley – for the man who has won the race, but declines to wear the laurels.'

Bentley buyers love spirited driving but tend to be understated people. An example is a famous industrial family who always opted for a Bentley. A US executive explained: 'When your name is DuPont, you don't need to raise your profile with a Rolls.'

Bentleys are regarded as the only cars in the world as good as a Rolls-Royce; hardly surprising, as for more than three-quarters of a century they were built by the same engineers and craftspeople.

For forty years, Fritz Fella's work embraced Bentley T, Continental convertibles, Silver Clouds, Shadows and Spirits. Chief engineer for styling and new model projects, he would describe the commitment of the highly skilled people behind the name to getting everything right. 'When you enter this car,' he told a journalist, 'you are in a different world … a remoteness from everyday cares.

'We are bound by tradition and are not revolutionaries in motor-car building. We are not interested in novelty, but the tried and true. We make changes only when the motor car will be improved and after 50,000 miles of testing.'

One example of innovation, he said modestly, led to Crewe engineers producing the first car with a heated rear window.

Before the Bentley Mulsanne arrived, Fritz reflected on the rules of the game: 'It must be a natural successor to our last car, maintaining identity and not merely by using a distinctive grille and bonnet mascot.'

The handsome Bentley T2 saloon, offering major technical advances on the S Series, enjoyed an exclusive position from 1965 to 1980, selling 2,272 over a fifteen-year production life. Basically, they were low-profile Rolls-Royce Silver Shadows.

The beautiful sweeping coachwork of the luxurious Bentley Corniche saloon. Only ninety-nine were built in the 1970s by the craftsmen at Mulliner Park Ward. Eager buyers compete whenever one comes up for sale.

Employing the best artisans to craft motor cars that were true to their heritage, Bentley and Rolls-Royce carved their own places at the top of the pyramid. As one journalist wrote, 'the exquisite craftsmanship … leather and wood set the tone for an unsurpassed travel experience … an all-round package that separates it from mere mortals.'

A Bentley is instantly recognisable and admired even by the many that have never driven in one. Various elements combine to create motor cars with a unique presence: understated but distinctive styling, allied to good taste – not an easily definable quality but recalling the saying, 'Not sure I can describe it, but I know it when I see it.'

Built largely by hand, a Bentley is a blend of form and function, brought together by talented craftspeople and engineers, dedicated to producing the finest motor cars human ingenuity can achieve. It is testament to their work that of the 90,000 or so Rolls-Royce and about 45,000 Bentleys built before the companies separated in 2003, about three-quarters are still running.

Quality has been the key factor at every step. Each car would take between three and five months to build, the assembly line moving just a few feet each day, and then only when the craftsmen were satisfied that the job had been done right. They initialed a history book accompanying each car that also recorded the materials used.

Did you know?
Bentley records are so comprehensive that a key can be cut without an original to copy for cars dating back to the 1960s.

A Bentley was made up of 80,000 components, many produced in the Crewe machine shop to ensure top quality, the aim being to ensure that the car would have several times the lifespan of other makes.

One engineer took final responsibility for each hand-built engine, which he ran for two hours, paying particular attention to quietness and vibration. A specialist listened for unusual noises with the end of a dipstick – as good as a stethoscope to his experienced ear. In addition, one in every hundred was put through a punishing twenty-hour test cycle, then stripped to the last nut and bolt, and every piece examined for signs of wear, each component being computer-checked against original drawings. The engine was then reassembled and sent to the production line.

A prototype of the legendary 6.75-litre engine that powered the cars for many years was run at full throttle for the equivalent of 40,000 miles and found to be working well within accepted tolerances.

◄ One of the fastest cars ever to bear the Bentley name emerged in 2007 – a car to excite the Bentley Boys. This was the Continental GTC, a high-performance, 12-cylinder, all-wheel luxury convertible with a top speed north of 190mph.

▼ Making sure that each wire is in the right place.

to punishing, extended, full-power tests that might have made those of most other cars blow up. At full throttle, the exhaust manifolds glowed red hot, reaching over 800°C. Engineers were proud that every engine of each Bentley Turbo R was able to take full throttle acceleration from the moment it went on the road, though this was not recommended.

▲ Hand-building the engine, the heart of the car. An engineer takes his time.

The company solemnly advised owners many years ago: 'Provided the engine is serviced and run on reputable fuel and oils with proper filtration and cooling, it will exceed 250,000 miles without the heads coming off for attention. Our engines regularly do just that.'

The turbocharged engines that transformed the marque in 1982 were subjected

Did you know?

Bentley statements sometimes were quite lyrical. Of the benefits to the driver of a Bentley Eight, the company observed: 'The possession of a Bentley has always been regarded as tacit evidence of its owner's distinctive taste and knowledge of motor cars. It confirms his appreciation of the power and pleasure afforded by the ownership of a car which is made as well as experience, skill and ingenuity allow.'

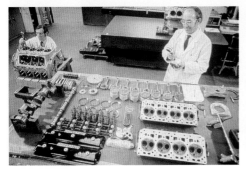

◄◄ Following bench-testing, one engine in a hundred is disassembled and checked for wear or imperfections.

◄ The history book chronicling every stage of manufacture.

The exhaust system was acoustically tuned to suppress a wide range of sound frequencies. During the 100-mile road testing, if a technician heard a sound that a roadside adjustment could not cure, he would send for a colleague with possibly the most acute hearing in the county. The colleague would climb into the boot, pull down the lid and lie with his ear to the carpeting, to identify the source.

Before other car makers even considered it, Bentleys had two and, for a time, three independent braking systems using discs and calipers of a size that would make you stare. If there was a failure, four-wheel stopping power was maintained, and the system would bring a car weighing more than 2 tons from 70mph to rest within four seconds. Later braking systems incorporated mineral oil, the hydraulic fluid used by Boeing to bring 747s to a stop.

A quiet interior has always been mandatory, even when accelerating to 100mph and beyond. Mulsanne Turbo

31

Only one hide in 100 passes the test as expert eyes look for blemishes or unacceptable marks. Rejects often wind up as expensive handbags.

without giving more than an inch. This test, however, was not advised by the company.

Anti-corrosive measures for each body shell required three days as several coats of epoxy-primers and black bituminous material were applied to the underside, which also helped to deaden sound.

The huge subframes were protected inside as well as out, inhibiting oil being sprayed through access holes which were then sealed.

Bentley has long been noted for the quality and richness of its colour schemes. The body is rubbed down several times between primers as the prelude to as many as fourteen coats of paint – an expensive commitment to a beautiful finish that will last for many years. Each coat is hand sprayed then hand rubbed before the next application, and the final protective coating is one and a half times thicker than that on most cars. To prove durability, painted

drivers were advised that they could go from 0 to 60mph in six seconds 'and still hear every word at 120 miles per hour'.

The hydraulic self-leveling suspension even took into account the emptying of the fuel tank. It was so strong, engineers claimed, that it would take the weight of a fully grown African elephant on the boot panels are taken to Australia to bake for days in the blistering outback, and to northern Scandinavia to see how they stand up to bitter winter exposure.

The double line running from the front to the back of the coachwork is applied by hand. It is fascinating to see a craftsman carefully dip a fine brush into the paint until he has just the right amount, squint along the car's waistline and, without pausing, apply two remarkably straight lines.

A Bentley is a beautifully designed and crafted mechanical device, but its heart and soul are the engineers and artisans who pour their talents into it and pass those skills on to their children. Bentleys are what they are because the company has always believed in uncompromising quality in everything it has ever done. That is why they perform so well and last so long.

From these sheets of rough-looking, paper-thin veneer, skilled craftsmen create the classic instrument panels and door cappings that set a Bentley apart from any other motor car.

Did you know?

When Bentleys were first exported to the United States, they were so quiet that the licensing authorities thought at first that they were powered by batteries rather than petrol engines

Vintage Bentleys and newer siblings. Enthusiasts drive great distances to this annual rally in Washington, in the north-western United States, to meet friends from all over the country and drive the cars. (All Sabu Advani)

The lusty cars for which Bentley became famous spawned a dozen or so playboy drivers who carved a niche in the 1920s – the distinction of being the best team of race drivers in the world. They beat everything the Germans, Italians or the French could offer and were known as the Bentley Boys. They were the motoring rock stars of the era, behaving like exuberant schoolboys, playing hard and inflicting punishment on the cars.

Well-heeled, they could indulge the good life in London's Mayfair and nightlife hot spots of Europe. Fast cars, silk scarves streaming in the breeze and a mistress here and there added to life's colour.

The Bentley Boys could have sprung from the pages of the weekly *Wizard* adventure paper devoured by schoolboys. Even their names fitted the lifestyle: Woolf Barnato, Sir Henry Birkin (known as Tim), Baron D'Erlanger, Glen Kidston, Bernard Rubin, S.C.H. 'Sammy' Davis, Dr J.D. Benjafield (a bacteriologist), Herbert Kensington-Moir, Frank C. Clement, L.G. Callingham, Jean Chassagne, George Duller, John F. Duff, and brothers Jack and Clive Dunfee. Four of them – Barnato, Birkin, Rubin and Kidston – owned adjoining apartments in Mayfair's Grosvenor Square, which cabbies knew as 'Bentley Corner'.

Most of them owned the cars they raced and often crashed. Woolf Barnato, their leader, was a likeable millionaire who had inherited a goldfield fortune and South African diamond mine. 'Babe', as he was known, had it all. Described by W.O. Bentley as 'the best British driver of his day', he bred horses, was a good boxer, golfer and cricketer, and raced speedboats and fast cars. With millions on tap, he lived a life few could imagine. But possibly most

> Woolf Barnato's Speed Six Bentley upset the French by outrunning the pride of French railways, 'The Blue Train'. The Bentley began in Cannes and arrived in London before the train reached Calais.

vital was racing for Bentley Motors, maker of robust grand tourers – thundering green warriors that were at home on the road or race tracks, which they dominated for a decade.

Three times he drove for the Bentley team in the famed Le Mans 24 Hours race, and each time was first at the finish. The racing was rough and physically demanding, heavy cars with unforgiving suspensions and no power assistance pushed to the limits. The experience in a 4½-litre Bentley was described by a journalist as 'not unlike riding on the footplate of a steam locomotive'. Little wonder, perhaps, that the Bentley Boys were known to take a shot or two of strong refreshment before the start.

Barnato was at a champagne dinner party in the South of France in 1930 when somebody said that a car had outrun the pride of French railways, 'The Blue Train', as it roared north. His favourite road car at that time was a Bentley Speed Six, 6½-litre coupé with Gurney Nutting coachwork that would write its own page in automotive history and forever be known as 'The Blue Train Bentley'. Barnato told the other guests that merely to go faster than the express was not difficult. A real test would be a long haul, and he bet £100 – a fair chunk of money in those days – that his Bentley Speed Six would get him to London before the train reached Calais. A friend who accepted the bet took the train and lost. Barnato left as the train pulled out of the station at 5.50 p.m. Driving fast on the *Route Nationale*, and despite fog, heavy rain and blowing a tyre, he caught the mid-morning cross-Channel ferry. By 3.20 p.m., he and a friend who'd come along as relief driver were having tea in a Conservative Club in London.

The Blue Train Speed Six, which Barnato had sketched on the back of an envelope,

◀ A friendly reminder to the French. The historic Speed Six with a special edition Arnage that was produced to commemorate the seventy-fifth anniversary of the Six's remarkable defeat of the French 'Blue Train'.

With one of their beloved Bentley racers (left to right), Sammy Davis, W.O. Bentley, Frank Clement, Dr J.D. Benjafield, L.G. Callingham and George Duller.

wasn't a handsome car. A steeply sloping back allowed only one rear seat to give access to the boot from the inside, along with picnic hampers and two cocktail cabinets – essential accoutrement for serious *bon vivant* travellers in those days. But the heart of the car was pure Bentley: a big engine that could take off in second gear and comfortably go straight into top. At Le Mans, Speed Sixes propelled the racers beyond 100mph. *The Autocar* magazine observed in September 1930 that the cars reacted immediately to the driver, 'suggesting the intelligence of an animal and giving just as much response to good treatment.

Did you know?

When the Bentley Mulsanne was introduced, only one body was required to pass United States stringent safety and impact testing, whereas most manufacturers use several. The car was crashed into concrete blocks at 30mph, front and rear, and dropped on its roof from several feet. It passed all the tests but was deemed not to be in saleable condition afterward.

'The Bentley feels that it is entirely under its driver's control with the minimum of effort whatever the speed, and however the road may twist or curve – a mysterious quality that makes one forget it is a machine.'

The roaring twenties were aptly named. Spectacular race-track success over ten years created the Bentley legend: big, aggressive cars attracting large crowds to Brooklands and Le Mans; winning the great 24 Hours endurance race five times; and doing much to establish the image of the Sarthe circuit as the place where the racing was exciting and drivers needed courage and strong nerves. It was tough and exhausting racing; furious driving for hour after hour, straining machines and drivers as they fought it out at high speeds through the night and into the next day. Collisions, brake failures, crashes, broken chassis and the occasional fire – it bordered on mayhem at times.

Battling European competitors – particularly German and French – Bentley won five times, four of which were in successive years from 1927 to 1930, which set a record unbeaten for thirty years.

Duff and Clement finished fourth in a 3-litre Bentley in the first Le Mans Grand

The 1930 Le Mans race 'do-it-yourself' pit crew. Barnato adds oil and Glen Kidston refuels their winning 6½-litre.

⋏ Bentleys taking first and second at Le Mans, 1930.

⋏➤ Commander Kidston and Captain Barnato lead the winners' parade. Note the cigarette being smoked by Kidston in those less politically correct days.

Prix d'Endurance in 1923 and won it the following year 10 miles ahead of the field, covering 1,290 miles in the twenty-four hours. A delighted British press trumpeted that they left forty rival French drivers in their wake. Three years later, in 1927, Benjafield and Davis drove a 4½-litre 1,472 miles to Le Mans victory – a consolation for Sammy who had crashed earlier.

The 1928 race, with three Bentley entries, was won by Barnato and Rubin, who held the lead for twelve hours. With speeds increasing, they clocked 1,658 miles. Tim Birkin set a 79mph lap record.

The year 1929 saw Bentley enter four standard production cars and win Le Mans for the third consecutive year. The Bentley Boys ran riot, finishing first, second, third and fourth. They held the first four places for eighteen hours, and Barnato and Birkin, driving a 6½-litre Speed Six, crossed the line first, having averaged 73.6mph over 1,767 miles. They were followed by three 4½-litres driven by Kidston and Jack Dunfee, Dr Benjafield and Baron d'Erlanger, and Clement and Chassagne.

By this time, Bentleys were scorching down the Mulsanne straight at 112mph, and they notched up their fifth Le Mans win with first and second in the 1930 race. Barnato won for the third year running. Glen Kidston was his co-driver in what was the last Le Mans appearance of a Bentley works team.

W.O. Bentley saw motor sports as a wonderful publicity tool for his cars, entering standard road Bentleys in motor-racing and hill-climb events to illustrate that a souped-up engine was unnecessary to prove utility and durability. A 3-litre,

however, was given a streamlined body to compete in the 1922 Indianapolis 500.

Bentleys were soon racing everywhere, such as for the Isle of Man Tourist Trophy and in punishing races at Brooklands, the home of British motor sport where Bentley himself was in the driving team and where

Le Mans – W.O. Bentley, J.F. Duff, Frank Clement and a 3-litre racer.

43

every production model was tested until 1929. Barnato and Jack Dunfee ran first in a 6½-litre in the 1929 Brooklands six-hour, and Frank Clement and Jack Barclay averaged 107mph in a 4½-litre to win the Brooklands 500. Sammy Davis, in a Speed Six, ran the fastest lap at 126mph. Barnato and Clement drove 2,080 miles at 86mph to win the Brooklands double twelve-hour in 1930, with Sammy Davis and Clive Dunfee right behind to take second. And

Bentley finished second, third, fourth, fifth, seventh and eighth in the Irish Grand Prix.

The mighty racers put down the marker that separated Bentley from the rest of the pack, despite talented drivers and very good cars being produced by the Germans and the French. Bentley, in just ten years, had carved an indelible niche in automotive history.

However, Bentley's top-quality engineering standards were costly; racing was expensive, and the 1929 Depression added

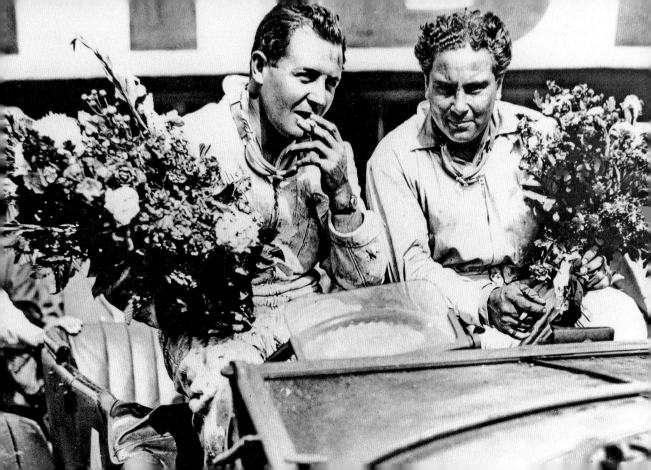

Tim Birkin in his 4½-litre Blower, with three wheels airborne, on the banking at Brooklands in 1932.

to a chain of financial difficulties. As befell many car companies over the years, Bentley, even at the height of its racing fame, ran into cash-flow problems. The flamboyant Woolf Barnato bailed out the ailing company, putting in £90,000 – a fortune in those days – and drove a hard bargain with shareholders, paying only 5 per cent of the value of their stock.

Friends swore that he came to the rescue only to ensure a supply of Bentleys to drive. In a five-year period, he owned twenty-three, including five 8-litres.

Barnato became chairman, ignoring those who said it was rash to get financially involved. Economic reality caught up, however, and in 1931 – just a year after their last Le Mans victory – large loans were called in which the company could not pay and Barnato declined to open his wallet again. He lost his big initial investment and a lot more cash he had provided to keep

Did you know?
An owner queried why sixty-four nuts under his car were painted yellow. He was told gravely that the nuts securing the body to its base subframes were tightened to a precise torque and painted so that unauthorised meddling or adjustments could be detected.

Bentley going. Typically, he shrugged it off, noting that he'd covered his losses on a diamond deal that very week.

Bentley Motors went into receivership, and Rolls-Royce bought the assets for £125,000, which included the services of W.O. Bentley, and a new Bentley Motors was formed as a Rolls-Royce subsidiary.

Racing Bentley comes home to the Brooklands banking.

Tim Birkin, joint winner with Woolf Barnato of the 1929 Le Mans race, takes the Pontilieue hairpin. This was the first year the 6½-litre Speed Six had raced and led Bentley to a historic victory, taking the first four places.

Walter Bentley created a legendary reputation in just a dozen years, producing 3,061 cars powered by 3-, 4½-, 6½- and, eventually, a massive 8-litre engine that offered 100mph motoring and outperformed the Rolls-Royce Phantom II.

The Bentley Boys raced for Bentley because they loved it. Apart from bragging rights, all they received was technical support and hotel rooms when racing. Over several years, they demolished the competition with great cars of speed, strength and endurance that prompted the Italian car maker Ettore Bugatti to comment: 'Mr. Bentley makes the fastest lorries in Europe.'

Lorries or not, Bentleys took on all comers and blew them away. Legends indeed!

Bentley drivers, for the most part, are sticklers for correctness. One, an American banker, has the distinction of being the first owner to write off a Turbo

R. William 'Bill' M. Davis is a courtly gentleman with a collection of eight classic cars, and for many years drove them 600 miles to the Albers Bentley service shop

Did you know?

A Bentley driver never saw ash when he opened the veneered ashtray in the centre console. It emptied automatically into a concealed bin. Lore has it that owners were advised to replace the car when the ash bin was found to be full.

➤ The Turbo R astonished the motoring world by achieving 0–60mph in 6.5 seconds – remarkable for a 2½-ton luxury car. It later became the flagship of the Bentley fleet. Pop stars and stock traders dreamed of owning one, and many did.

near Indianapolis, which enjoyed a stellar reputation.

En route to Indiana in a Turbo R – a quick machine that brought the schoolboy out in him – Bill skidded on a bend, crashed through a guardrail and hurtled down steep banking. He came out of it in better shape than the car, whose tank-like construction undoubtedly saved him. As he clambered out of the wreckage and gathered his senses, he saw that his jacket had flown out; his glasses too. A motorist peered over the demolished guardrail. 'Are you OK?' he called. 'Yes, I'm fine,' said Bill, 'but would you mind handing down my jacket?' A Bentley owner, he reasoned, could not possibly greet the constabulary or tow truck in a disheveled state. Bill fished out a pair of sunglasses in the centre console. Wearing the shades, and again sartorially elegant, he found it difficult to accept that he resembled a hip impersonator of an ageing Elvis after an energetic concert. His emergence from the wreck was done in style. But, of course, nothing less would be expected of a Bentley owner.

Bill bought another Turbo R with the new automatic ride control suspension – fast wheels for a banker. And he loved it. When we last met a few years ago, he noted that it had 143,000 briskly driven miles on the clock and was a joy to drive.

Former heavyweight boxing champion, Mike Tyson, going through a stressful

Did you know?

Bentley Motors sums up its array of stylish cars as 'sporting motor cars for serious drivers who demand performance, space and luxury'.

The substantial Arnage limousine – an ideal armoured car candidate.

period, was driving his $200,000 Bentley through Manhattan with his wife when they began to argue. He stopped the car, hailed a couple of policemen and said, 'Take it!' They did, and drove it to a garage in New Jersey. NYPD top brass were not amused.

A *New York Daily News* cartoon depicted Bentley directors in dark jackets and striped trousers collapsing in the boardroom. One – a Colonel Blimp-type character – is shown pounding his head on the desk, shouting, 'Some beastly colonial pugilist is giving them away!'

Mulliner Park Ward, the coachbuilding cathedral of bespoke craftsmanship, offers a range of beautifully designed additional features to meet the whims of owners who require a concealed cigar humidor or a mobile office where iPad, fax machine, television, fridge or cocktail cabinet glide silently behind veneered panels. One,

> Hand-crafted by Mulliner Park Ward master coachbuilders, this is the Bentley Continental – an elegant convertible combining graceful styling with supreme luxury. The body took several weeks to shape before being taken to Crewe for mechanical fitments. It was then returned to Mulliner Park Ward for interior furnishing and the fitting of the top.

Did you know?

The company developed the most advanced dual-level air conditioning for its 1980 models and proclaimed that you could drive a Bentley from the Arctic Circle to the Equator without adjusting the system. Once set, the car's temperature remained constant.

dazzled by the array of options for a Turbo R, added almost £50,000 to the price with a list of extras that took weeks to make. 'The Bentley Boys live,' mused the craftsmen.

Some requests almost defied imagination. A Los Angeles music industry executive ordered a stereo system so powerful that the speakers delivered enough decibels to

raise hair on the back of the neck. It set the owner back more than $30,000 and, when blasting away with the windows down, it could be heard on the next block.

A special service for nervous owners in recent years was a blast-proof car at prices of eye-watering proportions. Those, whose heads lay uneasily, could specify a 'protected car', as an armoured Bentley was discreetly described. In addition to a reinforced floor and doors that could withstand a hefty

Did you know?

A button converted the petrol gauge in the Bentley T saloon and in later models into an oil-level check. This avoided drivers having to use the dipstick – a convenience that also avoided gentlemen getting grime on their cuffs.

◄ The Bentley T, introduced in 1965, was virtually a technical revolution, with advanced systems like four-wheel disc-braking and independent suspension.

Did you know?

The climate-control system in the Bentley T, the most advanced in the world, had the heating capacity of four radiators and the cooling power of thirty refrigerators. It could also change the air in the car twice a minute.

explosion, survival features included an air supply to counter gas attacks; a mechanism to jettison thick windows for a quick exit; and an aggressive device to envelop the surrounding area in clouds of smoke. No one would confirm that the inspiration for some of these gadgets was the startling ejection seat in James Bond's Aston Martin in *Goldfinger*.

As terrorism concerns mounted, the Rolls-Royce/Bentley school of driving instruction expanded its curriculum for chauffeurs and skilled owner-drivers to encompass kidnap-evasion measures like high-speed reversing, braking and swing arounds.

◄◄ The refined rear interior cabin can accommodate hidden extras and special features.

◄ The 2013 Bentley Command Post. The world's finest upholstery, analogue instrumentation and brushed-steel features characterise Crewe artisans' workmanship.

Did you know?

The security system in the Bentley T2 was patterned after pin-tumbler locks designed in Egypt 4,000 years ago to protect the tomb of a pharaoh. The odds against a thief successfully forging a key was claimed to be 24,000 to 1.

This stylish car, introduced
in the early 1970s as
the Mulliner Park Ward
two-door saloon, became
the Bentley coupé,
which is much sought by
collectors today.

In the 1960s, Dr Adrian Rogers paid Bentley an unsolicited compliment: 'My S3 combines the sobriety required for my profession and the 100% reliability I need for night calls.' He practised in England in a time when doctors were still known to attend to a patient after hours.

When the Turbo R was introduced, potential buyers were given a first-hand taste of its scalding performance at a high-speed test track. Of course, they loved it, imagining they were the Bentley Boys of yore, thrilled to whizz around the banked circuit at something approaching

The good life. The annual rally of Bentley and Rolls-Royce aficionados in England is the largest in the world, with hundreds of motor cars often making the pilgrimage. This one attracted a record 1,200 cars to Castle Ashby, ancestral home of the Earl of Northampton. Owners and their families drive long distances for a day out, polishing their motor cars, picnicking and hoping for an award for the beauty and condition of their prized transport. (Christopher Abbiss)

140mph. That was until a tyre burst. The car cannoned off the guardrail and slewed around the banking until the test driver skilfully brought it to rest in the infield. 'The unscathed passengers staggered out of the half-wrecked car muttering "By jove I think I'm alive because I was in a Bentley".'

Impressed by the Turbo's handling and body strength, the delightful old boys wobbled away to drink a club toast to 'those splendid Bentley chaps who make such a jolly strong motor car'.

Good for a quick exit: the
Continental GT.

F Scott Fitzgerald commented: 'Let me tell you about the very rich. They are different from you and me.'

He was certainly right about the heavyweight champion of car collectors, His Majesty Sultan Haji Hassanal Bolkiah, head of the Brunei Royal Family. One of the world's richest men, with a 1,700-room palace and strong British connections, his oil-rich country bordering Malaysia generates about $2 billion a year for the family and he reportedly gave his daughter an Airbus for her eighteenth birthday.

A friend of Queen Elizabeth II and graduate of the military academy at Sandhurst, he has long been a fan of the finest British motor cars, owning about 350 Bentley and Rolls-Royce, along with Formula One championship-winning race cars and other exotic metal. In 1999 the Royal House of Brunei collection was listed by *Car and Driver* magazine at a staggering 5,000 cars. It includes unique handcrafted Bentley and Rolls-Royce models fitted with special engineering and luxury features. The Sultan insisted, in 1991, on having the very first Bentley Continental R coupé and paid more than £2 million for it. Scores of special cars were built for him, including the

In 1986, Graham Hull, chief stylist of Bentley and Rolls-Royce Motor Cars, drew this concept based on the Turbo R platform. It convinced the board to approve an exclusive Bentley coupé, which became the Continental R and thrilled enthusiasts all over the world.

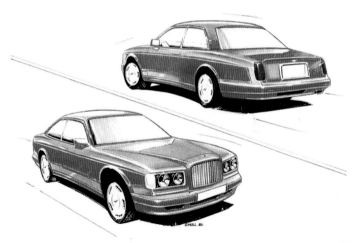

▶ The Continental R that emerged from the drawings.

only two six-door saloons ever produced at Crewe. Many other meticulously crafted models incorporating unique features occupied craftsmen for months and ran the bills into more than £1 million each.

The Sultan's orders, worth tens of millions, were crucial in keeping the company going in the early 1990s, when it was in financial

Did you know?
Wheel nuts and bolts of brass were made in-house at the Crewe factory to ensure not only top quality, but to create left- and right-hand threads to run counter to the direction of travel, so they would never work loose.

Classic Bentley: 1956 S1 Continental, admired the world over, inspired the drawing-board musings of later Bentley stylists.

PBC 666

Concept Java; this compact four-seat roadster never went into production – except for the Sultan, for whom several were made by hand.

Did you know?
The glass in every motor car is given its final polish with powdered pumice of a fineness normally used for polishing optical lenses.

trouble. More than £100 million from Brunei, including £30 million in one year, were a lifeline and helped finance future mainstream models.

It was generally believed that only one Bentley Java concept car was built: the stylish convertible/coupé with a removable hardtop that created a sensation at the

Did you know?

Hong Kong claims to have more Bentley and Rolls-Royce cars to the square acre than anywhere else, but for many years the tiny principality of Monaco claimed more per capita: 300 in a country the size of London's Hyde Park, with a population of 30,000.

◀ Java had a removable top to make it a coupé/convertible and interior styling cues of the Continental R were there: a console running to the rear, along with slim, Connolly leather sports seats. The car excited enthusiasts but was abandoned on financial grounds.

BENTLEY

◀ Touch of flamboyance – an eye-catching version of the Bentley Continental convertible.

➤ Magnificently crafted interiors captivated the Sultan, and helped generate millions of pounds' worth of orders.

Geneva motor show in 1994; it was used as a stalking horse to measure public reaction. The work of Graham Hull and Design Research Associates, Java never went into production because mainstream models had first call on development money. But the exciting small Bentley triggered worldwide publicity and, though the public never got to buy one, the Sultan certainly did. Several were built, each one yielding a handsome profit and bearing a plaque on the engine announcing that it was 'specially constructed for the Royal House of Brunei'.

In addition to hundreds of Bentley and Rolls-Royce in the vast Brunei collection, there are many more cars to make automotive buffs swoon: eight McLaren F1s, scores of Ferraris, Mercedes, Porsches, and more than 200 Aston Martins with special interior, engine and suspension features. Some have unique bodies like shooting brakes and coachwork by Italy's Pininfarina – another automotive enterprise that has happily enjoyed the indulgences of the House of Brunei.

Did you know?

The colder the climate, the better the leather! One reason for the superlative quality of the hand-cut and -sewn hides in a Bentley. Most are sourced in Scandinavia where pastures are not enclosed by sharp wire fencing so as to avoid scratches on the hides.

The Sultan deserves credit for ensuring that Bentleys continued to have British-built engines when Crewe, unable, in the 1990s, to afford the enormous cost of a replacement for its 6¾-litre V8, turned to BMW for the next-generation engine.

A controversial decision to put it mildly. However, the Sultan refused to have German engines for his cars, and given the critical cash flow from the Brunei order book, there was consternation in factory management. A way had to be found to give him the old, proven British engine, but doubts abounded that it would squeeze into the new Arnage and Seraph models.

The venerable 6¾-litre was boosted to 400hp and shoehorned into the Arnage. Once again, the Bentley radiator fronted an engine worthy of its heritage and the Arnage Red Label hit the spot for Bentley drivers. Thanks to the Sultan of Brunei, 'the old thunderer' was back – a real Bentley engine, built at Crewe where all Bentley engines should be made.

Walter Bentley's automotive and aviation engineering experience put him in lockstep with Henry Royce, and he could have contributed much when Bentley and Rolls-Royce came together in 1931. His engine design history and world-beating cars should have given him a leading role, particularly as Henry Royce was in failing health and died in 1933.

Bentley had a service contract but his talents were seldom tapped. Outside the mainstream, he was wasted on work that bore little relation to his engineering abilities – a puzzling misstep. By 1935 he had no meaningful input in Bentley Motors and left to design Lagonda and Aston Martin engines. He was 83 when he died in 1971. Hundreds made the pilgrimage to a memorial service at Guildford Cathedral in a Bentley car cavalcade of which sixty-eight were 40 years old or more.

Stanley Sedgwick, chairman of the Bentley Drivers Club, described W.O. as a quiet man who never sought the limelight, would not make a public speech and was embarrassed when Bentley car lovers thanked him for the pleasure he had brought to their lives. Few people were known widely just by their

▼ Eight-litre Bentley limousine, 1930 – one of the last original Bentleys prior to the company becoming part of Rolls-Royce.

▼ Bridging three-quarters of a century: a vintage Bentley 8-litre and new Mulsanne.

Did you know?

A Bentley has five and a half times as many components as the average car.

initials, but those of 'W.O.' would long be remembered and were enshrined in the cars that bore his name – cars that showed every sign of sharing the longevity of the man who conceived them.

The Rolls-Royce takeover heralded the end of Bentley's glorious racing era, though Barnato and the Bentley Boys continued, particularly at Brooklands, where they crashed fairly often between winning the 500 and Tim Birkin setting a 137mph lap record.

Absorbed into the Rolls-Royce culture, Bentleys continued to be produced and 2,432 were built at the Derby factory between 1933 and 1939, with 3½- and 4¼-litre engines designed to match the Rolls-Royce 25/30 model. Though bearing Bentley radiators, and known as 'Silent Sports Cars', they were not seen by buffs as true Bentleys. Now and again, however, there was a breakout with distinctive cars that reflected the DNA of the legend through the spectacular sweeping lines of the R-Type Continental and Flying Spur, and convertibles from coachbuilders Park Ward, H.J. Mulliner and James Young.

After the Second World War, car production moved to Crewe, in Cheshire, to a factory that had been built to make the Rolls-Royce

Did you know?

In the quest for quietness and smoothness, engineers at Crewe designed a unique electric gear selector. No push or pull was needed to engage drive or an intermediate gear. A slight pressure on the lever was sufficient for the transmission to respond without fuss or noise.

The 1953 R-Type's beautiful lines and distinctive sweeping tail, for which the car is famous. (Both Frank Allocca)

► Coach-built 1952 two-tone, four-door saloon, constructed on a Mark VI chassis. (W.O. Bentley Memorial Foundation)

►► *Olga*, a famous Bentley Continental sports saloon, 1951 prototype R-Type. Owned for many years by Stanley Sedgwick, president of the Bentley Drivers' Club. She has 375,000 miles on the clock and is considered now to be 'just nicely run in'. *Olga* can best 100mph quietly and serenely and has ride control, which offers soft motoring in the city and a firmer suspension for serious driving. (W.O. Bentley Memorial Foundation)

◄◄ The spectacular Bentley S1, sibling of the Rolls-Royce Silver Cloud, which is viewed by many to be the company's most beautiful car.

◄ The Bentley T2, introduced in 1977, had tighter suspension and steering, and promised Bentley aficionados luxury, speed, safety, smoothness and silence, along with the cachet of a sporting pedigree.

Merlin engine for the RAF Spitfires and Hurricanes that defeated the Luftwaffe in the Battle of Britain. Car engines later benefited from precision machinery accurate to one-ten-thousandth of an inch, which engineers said explained why a Bentley engine should take 200,000 miles in stride.

The company decided to go beyond making just the chassis and running gear, and build the complete car. The first

Did you know?

The Bentley exhaust system was acoustically tuned to suppress a wide range of sound frequencies, and every motor car was road tested for 100 miles to ensure that the sound-proofing met company standards for quiet, restful travel.

standard steel-bodied post-war Bentley was the 4¼-litre 6-cylinder 1946 Mark VI saloon.

Six years later, two classic Bentleys were launched: the Flying Spur four-door saloon and the R-Type Continental, a graceful two-door fastback with light alloy bodywork by coachbuilders H.J. Mulliner. The R-Type was the first automatic-transmission Bentley and the world's fastest four-seat production sports saloon whose tuned 4¾-litre engine could sustain 120mph.

These luxurious silent sports cars hinted that Bentley could carve a new niche and have greater relevance, even if a renaissance for the great marque was just a gleam in the eyes of Bentley lovers in the company.

The S1, in 1955, was a handsome Bentley companion to the Silver Cloud, whose stylish, flowing lines led to it being hailed as the most beautiful Rolls-Royce ever. They were the last cars with separate chassis and bodies to be manufactured at Crewe.

'Badge engineering'. Though the Mulsanne bore a Bentley grille, it was a Rolls-Royce Silver Spirit in most respects. But it was hailed as 'the return of the silent sports car' and targeted motorists who wanted a sporting driving machine image, yet still enjoy the quality and luxury of a Rolls-Royce. (Christopher Abbiss)

⬆ One of the early Bentleys built by Rolls-Royce: 1934 Derby Bentley with coachwork by Freestone and Webb. (W.O. Bentley Memorial Foundation)

➤ Mark VI chassis, two-door coachwork by James Young. Just eight were made in this body style. (Alan Bodfish)

Built for just over ten years, the S Series, crafted with the finest veneers, Connolly leather and Wilton carpeting, captivated Bentley followers. By 1959, the S2 had an alloy 6¼-litre V8, automatic transmission and power steering, and three years later became the S3, a grand touring luxury car. Revered for their beauty to this day, the S and Silver Cloud sold 14,909 between 1955 and 1966. Half, including coach-built Continentals, were Bentley.

In 1965, radical styling and engineering improvements marked the new T Series. It had a monocoque steel body that distributed stress over the entire skin instead of a traditional chassis frame, and the doors,

Built in Bentley's heyday – 1925
3-litre open tourer. Note the handbrake
on the outside. (Marian Savage)

Vanden Plas body – 1929 4½-litre
Bentley and its engine. (Both Frank
Allocca)

bonnet and boot lid were aluminium. A two-door coupé and a convertible followed within a couple of years.

Though lower and more compact than the S Series, the T was roomier with technical innovations like automatic air conditioning, rack and pinion steering, self-levelling independent front and rear suspension, and a back-up braking system.

Two thousand changes and improvements were engineered into the T Series over a fifteen-year lifespan in which Bentley retained its exclusivity, selling 2,420. Meanwhile, the Rolls-Royce Silver Shadow, Wraith and Corniche, which shared the same body styles, had a production run of about 30,000.

When a handsome successor emerged in 1980 it was given a name rather than a letter or number. Called Mulsanne, after the famous straight at Le Mans, it was the most sophisticated Bentley to date, and signalled the beginning of historic change for the marque.

The genesis of a Bentley revival took hold in the early 1980s. David Plastow, who joined the company as a young sales rep and progressed to Rolls-Royce Motor Cars managing director, was sure there were people out there who enjoyed spirited driving and would buy a luxurious performance car but felt they were too young for an establishment image. He proposed recasting Bentley, capitalising on the racing history, but development costs ruled out a separate range of dedicated Bentleys.

Taking three months to handcraft each car was the opposite of economy of scale, hence severe financial constraints, but Plastow asked Engineering and Styling to make a serious effort to energise the Bentley image. Their creativity triggered a renaissance that became critically important to the company's survival a few years down the road. It began with the Bentley Mulsanne, a Rolls-Royce Silver Spirit fronted by a Bentley radiator.

The Mulsanne, drawing on Bentley heritage, had been positioned as a saloon of impeccable road manners, fastidious attention to detail, silent and comfortable

In the mid-1980s, Project 90 – dubbed 'the Black Rat' – excited aficionados and, although it did not go into production, heralded Bentleys to come with distinct separation from Rolls-Royce models.

In the early 1980s, the Mulsanne Turbo signalled that performance was back for Bentley.

stretch. Crewe cars were seen as having the wind resistance of the Hoover dam.

Aerodynamics became academic, however, and 1982 was a milestone marking a significant move that redefined Bentley's identity and offered drivers greater substance than just badging.

A Garrett turbocharger was matched to the powerful 6¾-litre engine to generate stunning, yet smooth acceleration to pin your ears back. The car got a new name – Mulsanne Turbo – its performance hitting 110mph before the base Mulsanne could

– the newest of a historic line of cars that had made Bentley a byword for enthusiastic drivers for more than half a century. But any inference that it zipped along more sportingly than a Rolls-Royce was illusory. The Mulsanne was a little wider and lower than its T2 predecessor to make it more aerodynamically efficient. That idea was a

Did you know?
Test drivers clocked 1 million miles in a year in the Bentley Mulsanne and its turbocharged version, which heralded the revival of the Bentley marque in the 1980s.

> Bentley Eight, the foundation for a new breed, had its California launch alongside another British icon, the *Queen Mary*. Eight had the characteristics of a driver's car, but at a more affordable price and attracted new customers. A wire-mesh grille was a reminder of the glory days of Le Mans.

reach 90mph. This decidedly was not your father's Bentley. It was hailed as 'the return of the silent sports car, a fast sporting machine – the latest statement of the Bentley philosophy'.

But it needed a firmer suspension to improve corner handling while retaining ride quality, and this was a priority for a visionary new engineering director, Michael Dunn, when he arrived from Ford in 1983. A softly spoken man who looked more like a banker than somebody who would push a car to its limits on a test track, Dunn spearheaded technical improvements that

developed the Mulsanne Turbo into a car to thrill the Bentley Boys.

It was renamed the Bentley Turbo R – the R for road-holding – and it was a game-changer: a full-blooded four-door hot-rod of phenomenal power. It propelled its 2½ tons from 0 to 60mph in six seconds and could top 135mph. Launched in 1985, the R was faster than any Bentley had ever been. Journalists dubbed it, 'Crewe's Missile – the car that gave Bentley back its dignity'. Traditionally, the company declined to quote horsepower, merely describing performance as 'sufficient'. So great was speculation about the enormous power of the Turbo R, however, that the Bentley

◄ With the convertible hood raised, the Bentley Continental looked just like a hard-top coupé, testament to the skills of the coachbuilders at Mulliner Park Ward.

The Mulsanne – a new body style – with many technical improvements, was introduced in the early 1980s; it was then turbocharged and became a significant signal that the Bentley range was about to expand into the high-performance market.

▶ Champagne toast by the Bentley crew when the Turbo R broke sixteen speed records, covering more than 140 miles in one hour at the Millbrook circuit in England.

spokesmen deigned to murmur 'sufficient, plus fifty per cent'.

Richard Perry, managing director of Bentley and Rolls-Royce, a former navy pilot with a taste for speed, and Peter Ward, the marketing director who also pursued fast driving, energetically encouraged Bentley development, and Ward chortled that the Turbo R would 'blow the doors off most Porsches'.

Bentley fans marvelled when a production Turbo R, at the Millbrook circuit in Bedfordshire, set sixteen speed records – some of which had stood for fifty years. Test driver Derek Rowland completed each 2-mile lap in less than fifty-two seconds, recapturing for Bentley the British International one-hour endurance record, covering more than 140 miles and beating by 8 miles the record held by a Lamborghini Countach. Bentley was reclaiming its heritage.

Meanwhile, the Bentley Eight had been launched the previous year to attract entry-level buyers – young, affluent achievers reaching for the best of sports motoring. With a firm suspension, a striking bright wire-mesh grille reminiscent of the Le Mans racers and a 6¾-litre engine taking it to 100mph very quickly, it had fewer top-of-the-line refinements like patterned walnut, but it was sporty, less costly than the Mulsanne and was a ticket to the luxury club.

A convertible, identical to the Rolls-Royce Corniche apart from a Bentley radiator, was renamed. The Bentley Continental convertible became an exclusive alternative to the high-profile Rolls-Royce Corniche in Beverly Hills and similar habitats of the seriously rich. It was billed as a classic luxury sporting convertible, offering two worlds: top-down motoring with sports-style seats and a quiet coupé when the weather was less than kind. An elegant car, flawlessly crafted and requiring five months to build, had classic lines that were testament to the skills of the craftsmen coachbuilders at Mulliner Park Ward, who shaped the metal and veneered wood trim and tailored the finest hides, rich carpeting and lambswool rugs of cars that, for many, were what dreams were made of. The expensive and time-consuming process took one

craftsman a week to fit the convertible top – work of such art that, when raised, the car appeared to be a coupé.

'All Bentley, all the time' might have been the slogan, as a concept study (Project 90), hinting at a separate body for a Bentley, appeared in 1985. Dubbed 'the Black Rat', it was a big two-door with a long bonnet and flowing side panels, and it created a buzz. However, it fell short of the stylish Continental of yesteryear, and chief stylist Graham Hull came up with a more appealing concept: a sleek, eye-catching coupé that became the Continental R – the first Bentley in forty years not to share a body style with Rolls-Royce.

It created a sensation at the Geneva show, when it was unwrapped in 1991 as 'the sporting supercar', and stole all the international publicity, to the chagrin of some German manufacturers.

A year's production was sold out before the first Continental R left the factory. The car was elegant with a luxurious leather and veneered interior, a flow-through centre console for a cockpit effect and technical advances like electronic ride control that switched from soft to firm in an instant.

The magic of Brooklands, the cradle of British motor racing. Bentley took its new model, named in honour of the famed circuit, to what remained of the banking that challenged the Bentley Boys in the 1920s and 1930s. The Brooklands saloon is seen below with a classic Bentley racer that has seen more sweat, strain and race-track mayhem than the saloon drivers could imagine.

Performance was spectacular: rest to 60mph in 6.6 seconds and 145mph top speed, achieved, as the company said, 'with refinement and barely a whisper'. Trumpeted as 'the world's finest sporting coupé' – big, comfortable and very powerful – it sealed the renaissance.

Next came the Brooklands, a luxurious sporting saloon of 1993, introduced, appropriately, at Brooklands in Surrey, nearly three-quarters of a century after the Bentley Boys shattered speed records at the famous circuit and where Bentley

Did you know?

Craftsmen always acknowledged the past while looking to the future. In the early 1970s, Charles W. Ward, director of Mulliner Park Ward coachbuilding division, said: 'We are moving toward light alloy aircraft-type construction although our craftsmanship is inherited from the days of coaches drawn by six horses with postillions in knee breeches.'

The Turbo R 'Crewe's Missile' – the spectacular performance car that signalled to the motoring world that Bentley was back. Its 6¾-litre engine would move its 2-plus tons from 0 to 60mph in six seconds.

dominated racing for so many years. Walter Bentley drove his first race there in 1909.

Most of the old banking had crumbled over decades, but a small section remained and it was there that journalists heard the approaching roar of an engine of a long-gone era. The clock rolled back fifty years as a legendary racer came into sight: the 4½-litre Bentley that Woolf Barnato named *Mother Gun* and in which he and Bernard Rubin won Le Mans in 1928. The car held the record for the fastest speed over 1,000 miles of any Bentley, and clocked 131mph at the final Brooklands race meeting in August 1939. Now, this historic racer proudly led the newest expression of the Silent Sports Car – three Brooklands abreast, steadily holding position on the banking. Even the reporters applauded. Journalists generally do not do that.

The second new Bentley to be launched in eighteen months, the Brooklands blended superb handcrafting with advanced technology and was the first to be produced under more efficient manufacturing systems in which the company had invested £300 million.

The Brooklands superseded the Mulsanne. Though not turbocharged, it had sharp performance and technology such as automatic ride control to give it sports-car handling. With a long wheelbase version and tweaked performance, it began to take sales away from the Turbo R in the mid-nineties, being seen by buyers as probably the best value offered by the company. It added further heft to the Bentley revival, and not just among Bentley fans. One third of Brooklands buyers in its first year were Mercedes and BMW owners.

Bentley momentum had gathered pace in Britain and Europe, accounting for nearly half of production, but in the United States, the marque was virtually under the radar.

Most customers in the US super-rich league opted for a Rolls-Royce, so a programme was devised to highlight Bentley and its sporting history, and prepare the way for the mighty Turbo R, whose arrival had been delayed by US engine emissions rules.

The Mulsanne S was launched in New York as a performance five-seat luxury car with European handling and an engine with 18 per cent more power. It was targeted toward business people in their thirties and forties. The Continental convertible also got the more powerful engine, making it possibly the most luxurious top-down car on the road, and the ground was now ready for the Turbo R. Test drivers took journalists on fast white-knuckle trips in New Jersey's Meadowlands and when television reports showed the car's stunning performance, Bentley awareness spiked and sales took off in America.

The 1993 model year was a Bentley cavalcade, with six new models: Brooklands and a long wheelbase version; the flagship Continental R coupé; Turbo R plus a long wheelbase version; and the Continental convertible. The United States had never seen such a comprehensive Bentley range and sales overtook Rolls-Royce.

Another concept Bentley, code-named Java – a twin-turbo four-passenger coupé with removable top – was unveiled at Geneva in 1994. Again there was worldwide publicity and many plaudits, but the economics did not add up and it was quietly dropped.

However, it did add further interest to the Bentley revival and prepared the way for the Azure, which completed the Bentley blitz in 1995. A high-performance car and the first new-production Bentley convertible in a quarter of a century, it was named after the skies of the Cote d'Azur, and its stylng captivated the cognoscente. At $319,000, it was the most expensive car the company had ever offered in North America.

The elegant Continental R, the 'sporting super car', a classic coach-built performance coupé – the first Bentley in forty years not to share its styling with a Rolls-Royce.

Did you know?

Engineers, in the 1970s, devised an almost fool-proof car theft security system. The only way to steal a Bentley without the key was via tow truck. When the ignition key was removed, the transmission automatically locked in park.

It was shown at events in New York, Beverly Hills, Las Vegas and Palm Beach, where you can smell the money all around you, and like the Continental R in Europe, the first year's allocation sold out almost immediately.

In the mid-1990s, Bentley's six technically advanced models offering luxury, exclusivity, performance and heritage attracted new owners, particularly those whose advancing years made it difficult to squeeze into their Porsche or Ferrari.

The faith and skills of the Bentley pioneers at Crewe blossomed into an unprecedented range which generated much-needed cash. Bentley sales in 1984 were 212 – a modest fraction of the dominant Rolls-Royce. By the 1990s they had soared fivefold to 1,100 and were outselling Rolls-Royce.

The sales map had been turned upside down in North America and Europe. Bentley had become the exciting, rejuvenated prodigal son and was welcomed home. It was Rolls-Royce Motor Cars' financial saviour, but sadly not for long. By itself, it could not stave off financial pressures that led to the company being sold and the marques going to German ownership.

A confluence of events led to Rolls-Royce and Bentley Motor Cars separating after a fight for control between BMW and Volkswagen.

The 'wind in your hair' Azure luxury convertible of the mid-nineties attracted a huge order book in the US.

With an eye to the support of a strong parent company, chief executive David Plastow merged Bentley and Rolls-Royce in 1980 with Vickers, the tanks, guns and planes conglomerate. He became Vickers CEO and brought a cash cow with him as car sales hit records, increasing to more than 3,000 a year. For several years, they were the group's biggest profit earner as the Bentley surge gained momentum.

However, to bolster dividends, Vickers siphoned off money needed for investment in new models, and the car makers struggled to finance new technology and stay relevant.

Engineering director Michael Dunn told the board they had to tap into the mainstream motor industry and even partner with a major manufacturer, and he began to develop engineering links with BMW.

The Bentley boost eased financial pressures for several years until sales collapsed in the early 1990s as Europe, the US and the Far East dived into recession. Every international market tanked, sales plunged by more than half – the worst for more than twenty years – and red ink splashed everywhere. The factory workforce was cut by half as losses in 1991 exceeded £100 million and Vickers itself came close to going under, having to find £400 million to modernise production processes and cut costs. Car-build time was reduced from twelve to eight weeks while protecting traditional handcrafting, and as the recession eased, business picked up with a range of new and freshened Bentleys and revitalised Rolls-Royce models.

The signs, however, were undeniable. Just as Jaguar had needed the broad shoulders of a big parent to ensure survival,

The Crewe factory, now exclusively Bentley, was home to both Bentley and Rolls-Royce from 1945 until the marques separated in 2003. Volkswagen has transformed the former aero-engine plant into a high-tech automotive factory now producing some of the world's most powerful and luxurious sporting cars.

so too did Bentley and Rolls-Royce Motor Cars. Vickers, reeling from financial pain, looked for a buyer.

A ridiculous £150 million low-ball offer from BMW was rejected by David Plastow. He had steered the company through two successful decades and was not interested in a fire sale. However, in 1997, after Plastow's retirement, BMW tried again with a £340 million offer, which was accepted, triggering fierce objections from war veterans and some shareholders imploring Vickers not to sell to the Germans.

Then the sleeper, Volkswagen, came up on the rails, weighing in with £479 million, which Vickers agreed to. This infuriated BMW and started a corporate brawl between the chairmen, BMW's Bernd Pischetsrieder and Volkswagen's Ferdinand Piech.

At a shareholders' meeting to approve the deal in June 1998, a group of enthusiasts led by Michael Shrimpton, a Bentley-

owning lawyer, tried to keep the company British-owned but could not stitch financing together in time to top Volkswagen's offer. Their request for more time was rejected.

➤ The Arnage – a different car when the BMW engine was abandoned and the venerable 6¾-litre Crewe-built engine substituted. *Below*: The Crewe styling studio where a clay model turns drawings into a full-size car mock-up.

It was a raucous gathering, erupting at times in nationalistic fervour. Shareholders berated the directors for selling out a British icon to a foreign company. The *Financial Times* described the stormy meeting as 'a smouldering mix of petty jingoism and rampant corporate egos'.

Though Volkswagen's higher offer had been approved, BMW did not give up. It had two trump cards. If it did not get the right to make Rolls-Royce cars, Pischetsrieder threatened to stop supplying engines and other parts for the new Silver Seraph and Bentley Arnage, which had been commissioned due to lack of development

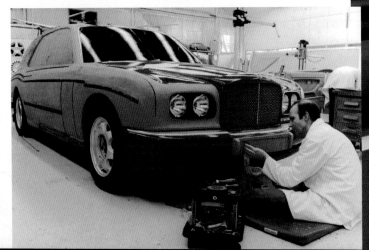

money. BMW also had business links to Rolls-Royce plc, the aerospace group that owned the Rolls-Royce name and RR badge and held the power to decide who could make cars bearing the trademarks. It decided in BMW's favour.

Volkswagen had assumed that Vickers had the right to permit it to make cars bearing the Rolls-Royce name. Vickers thought so, too. That turned out not to be the case. Faced with having a car that could not be called Rolls-Royce, and the considerable handicap of not having an engine, Piech agreed to hand over the Rolls-Royce name to BMW five years later.

BMW paid £40 million to the aerospace group for the right to use the Rolls-Royce name on cars it would assemble at a factory in the south of England.

Volkswagen's Ferdinand Piech was magnanimous, despite being shabbily blindsided. His purchase of Bentley and the Crewe factory included ownership of the iconic Rolls-Royce radiator and Flying Lady mascot, which he gracefully allowed BMW to use. He was acknowledged in the press as the only statesman in the whole acrimonious affair.

Volkswagen came away with Bentley and the factory, which it transformed, investing £1 billion, and continued to make Rolls-Royce models alongside Bentley until BMW assumed the name for its cars in 2003.

Volkswagen also secured the most valuable of all the Crewe resources: the renowned artisans whose skills had crafted motor cars of unparalleled quality for generations. They stayed put with Bentley in Cheshire, ignoring invitations to relocate to the south of England. They were, and remain, the bedrock of a new Bentley generation.

The new Bentley Motors got busy producing a stylish range of 'sporting

◀ The highly skilled craftsmen and women of Crewe make what most people believe are the finest interiors in the world.

motor cars', benefiting from Volkwagen's tremendous engineering heft as well as traditional Crewe luxurious interiors – a combination to ensure the future of a great marque.

The separation turned out to be a boon for both Bentley and Rolls-Royce.

The Azure T2 and the last in the works at Crewe – a final flourish with graceful styling and beautifully crafted interior.

After the struggle for control between the German industrial titans, Volkswagen was in an unusual position in 1998. Its focus was Bentley but also it had responsibility for Rolls-Royce until BMW assumed that role five years on. This left two final Crewe models, the Silver Seraph and a new Corniche convertible. They were beautiful cars of supreme quality – a last tip of the hat to Rolls-Royce from Crewe designers and engineers.

Before the Teutonic brawl, work had begun on a replacement for the 17-year-old body used by Mulsanne, Turbo R and Brooklands. Graham Hull and his design team produced the Arnage, a stylish four-door with soft, graceful lines. It was named after the challenging corner at Le Mans, and was launched there, in the heartland of Bentley's greatest racing successes, in April 1998, seventy years after Barnato and Rubin's 1928 Le Mans victory in a 4½-litre.

Arnage, with the first complete body built at the Crewe factory, had adaptive suspension and stability control, high-tech instruments and the first engine developed just for Bentley in nearly sixty years –

Did you know?
Bentley Motors describes its owners as 'individualistic as the cars they drive. They value a distinctive and thoroughbred sporting car which combines performance, security, smoothness, silence and space.'
A solar-gain instrument near the windscreen even adjusted the system to allow for the heat of the sun.

> A new Bentley powerhouse that would have thrilled the Bentley Boys: the Continental GTC, a high-performance 12-cylinder, four-wheel-drive convertible with a blistering top speed north of 3 miles per minute.

an aluminium alloy 4½-litre V8 with twin Cosworth turbochargers. Despite the work of Crewe and BMW engineers, its 350hp fell short of the performance Bentley drivers expected and sales picked up only when the engine was replaced by the big 6¾-litre that had powered Bentleys for many years. Renamed Arnage Red Label, it became stable mate to the Continental R and T coupés, and the Azure convertible.

Did you know?

Bentley commitment: 'Scrupulous attention is paid to every factor which affects the driver's physical and psychological equilibrium.'

Though decks were now clear for a new generation of Bentleys, Volkswagen managers, sensitive to heritage, took care not to meddle with the DNA. Changes that might dilute the 'Englishness' could contaminate the essence.

The factory was modernised, with tens of millions of pounds invested in robotics for the grunt work, while craftsmanship was carefully nurtured. No attempt was made to cut back the 200 hours spent on meticulously handcrafting veneered panels, leather upholstery and other interior work for each car. Craftsmen and women, whose measuring instruments were hand and eye, were left alone to apply skills handed down in their families.

Manufacturing efficiencies almost tripled output and the new faces of Bentley emerged, different in shape and performance, bearing historic names like Continental and Flying Spur. They were, and are,

◀◀ The Bentley State Limousine, presented to Queen Elizabeth II to mark the Golden Jubilee, took two years to build and had armour plating and bulletproof windows.

◀ Two Bentley race cars covered 3,196 miles and came first and second in the Le Mans 24 Hours endurance race, seventy-three years after the last Bentley win in 1930. First place No. 7 was driven down the Champs Elysees at the head of a cavalcade of vintage and current Bentleys.

phenomenally fast, capable of 180mph – some north of 200mph – which may qualify as overkill for road cars.

A 6-litre 550hp twin-turbo Bentley Continental GT sports coupé attracted hundreds of orders before production started in 2002. Journalist Phil Llewellyn commented: 'The new Bentley wunder-wagen is a technological tour de force … represents terrific value for money at the big-bucks end of the market … muscular and purposeful.'

As Volkswagen immersed itself in Bentley culture, it made two notable high-profile moves. A foothold was secured in the Buckingham Palace limousine fleet, traditionally monopolised by Rolls-Royce Phantoms. The Queen's 2002 Golden Jubilee was marked with the first Bentley State Limousine, a 3½-ton behemoth nearly 3ft longer than the Arnage and more than a ton heavier. The additional weight was due to hefty armour-plating. Press questions were met with, 'The nature of security equipment fitted is not for public consumption' – a lofty phrase to place alongside another Crewe stiff-lip classic: 'To speak of money is vulgar.' The Royal limo scored another first: it was presented to the Queen at Windsor Castle by a German, Franz-Josef Paefgen, the Bentley Motors chairman and chief executive. Though more technically sophisticated than the older Phantoms, it bore a large Bentley

Bentley returned to motor sport in 2013 with the 600hp twin-turbo GT3, here at the Goodwood Festival of Speed.

The flowing lines of the Bentley Arnage recalled styling cues from the legendary S1 and Silver Cloud.

radiator which some felt did not look quite as imposing as the commanding Royce grille and Spirit of Ecstasy mascot.

On a PR roll, Bentley's new owners, hoping perhaps to recapture some of the marque's lost soul, paid homage to illustrious history with a generous tribute to W.O. and his great drivers by recalling Le Mans glory seventy-three years earlier. Team Bentley – two sleek, low-slung, 600hp race cars with Flying B decals – won the 2003 Le Mans 24 Hours race, averaging 133mph over 3,196 miles. They finished first and second, and with that Bentley drivers were back on the podium.

It was a thrilling event with a commercial payoff: 3,500 orders poured in for the new Continental GT, making it the most successful Bentley ever sold, and it was followed by the GTC 2x2 convertible, a 12-cylinder 198mph projectile. By 2005, another legendary name, the Continental Flying Spur, was attached to a 195mph four-door, which quickly built a two-year order book.

The factory worked flat out; sales gathered pace, breaking 8,000 and then touching an unprecedented 10,000 in 2007, after which the recession put even the very wealthy on the defensive.

Bentleys outsold the BMW-made Rolls-Royce Phantom by several to one, but it should be noted that BMW was not allowed to launch a Rolls-Royce before 2003, which gave Volkswagen a five-year start.

Did you know?

20,000 solar panels covering much of the roof at the Crewe factory generate enough energy to power 1,200 houses for a year.

Special edition Arnage at Le Mans, birthplace of its name, to commemorate racing victories.

The 2007 Bentley Brooklands – the second model to bear the name of the racing circuit.

Two decades on, a new Mulsanne echoes Le Mans.

As Bentley Motors got into stride, revamping the factory, strengthening engineering and design, and making the name a meaningful player again in the luxury league, the range expanded with a special-feature Mulliner Arnage, and in 2007, a new Brooklands: a rakish two-door to mark the centenary of the famous racing circuit. The latter was propelled by the most powerful V8 engine in Bentley history. Barnato, Birkin and their racing pals would certainly have approved of that.

The Brooklands was followed by a stylish convertible, the Continental GTC, to celebrate the diamond anniversary of car making at Crewe. The mantra required supreme luxury and high performance, and by 2007, the 202mph Continental GT Speed hit the market, followed two years later by the Continental Supersport, which was a fraction faster. These stupefying cars are capable of covering a football field in about one second. It is to be hoped that the drivers are up to it.

AutoWeek described the turbocharged 4-litre 500hp Continental GT in 2012 as 'speed, effortlessness and understated excess that a Bentley represents'. It was heavy at just over 5,000lb, cost £100,000 and did 21mpg.

Fourteen years into the new generation, Bentley offered a range of cars with beautiful lines and rich interiors that shouted good taste (*sotto voce*, of course), bristling with technology to make even a techie's mind swim. With adaptive suspensions, stability controls, electronics and communications, drivers might find a degree in applied sciences useful.

Tuition in handling a car able to cover more than 3 miles in sixty seconds could be a life preserver for somebody testing the 225mph 2013 Continental GT Speed – the fastest Bentley production car. With a hint

of 1950s Continental R-Type styling, its 6-litre 616hp twin-turbo engine rockets to 60mph in four seconds – very quick for a 5,100lb car. Other irrelevant numbers for the rich: 15mpg and $226,000 with tax.

The 2014 Flying Spur, whose 625hp makes it the most powerful car in Bentley history, tops out at 200mph. A 6-litre, twin-turbo, 12-cylinder engine takes it from 0–60mph in 4.3 seconds, which is remarkable for a car weighing nearly 3 tons. Approaching 200mph, the air suspension lowers ride height to compensate for aerodynamic forces. No advice, though, on where it might be safe to drive it, or the Continental GT Speed, to the red line. In China, where most Flying Spur owners prefer to be driven, the car costs an eye-popping £400,000 with import duty.

A growing interest in returning to motor sport was underlined by the appearance of the Continental GT3 race car at the 2013 Goodwood Festival of Speed. More than 2,000lb lighter than a road GT, its race-tuned twin-turbo 4-litre V8 produced 600hp and was the work of a dedicated facility at Crewe.

In 2014, proclaiming that one in four luxury cars delivered worldwide was now a Bentley, the company announced record sales, 10,120 cars in twelve months and profit up 66 per cent to £139 million. A 193-strong dealer network in fifty-four countries had expanded in the Americas, the Pacific Rim and across Europe, opening up Russia and old Eastern Bloc countries.

With the flagship Flying Spur accounting for 25 per cent of sales, exports exceeded £1 billion, the US taking 31 per cent, China 22 per cent and Britain, despite a bumpy economy in recent years, buying 14 per cent.

Though the German takeover of two iconic British companies was controversial in Britain, reservations have softened with time. Volkswagen and BMW's huge investment and commitment are acknowledged, and it is accepted that had they not come along Bentley and Rolls-Royce might not be around today.

Heritage and time-honoured craftsmanship are being preserved, and the future would seem to be assured for the qualities and engineering excellence associated with Rolls-Royce and Bentley cars. A good deal for everybody, not least boy racers!

Doubtless, W.O. Bentley and the Bentley Boys would be very happy about that.

A 1930 4½-litre supercharged Bentley, with more than 100,000 miles under her wheels, being prepped at Crewe in 2013, prior to competing in the gruelling 1,000-mile Mille Miglia event. The car is one of two owned by Bentley Motors that have competed three times in Mille Miglia in recent years.

UU 5872

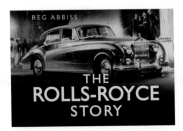

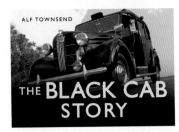